50 HAPPENS

Written By:
Herbert Kavet

Illustrated By:
Martin Riskin

To Marshall
Happy Birthday
Love
Harry & Lis

Ivory Tower Publishing Co., Inc.
125 Walnut St., Watertown, MA 02172
Telephone #: (617) 923-1111   Fax #: (617) 923-8839

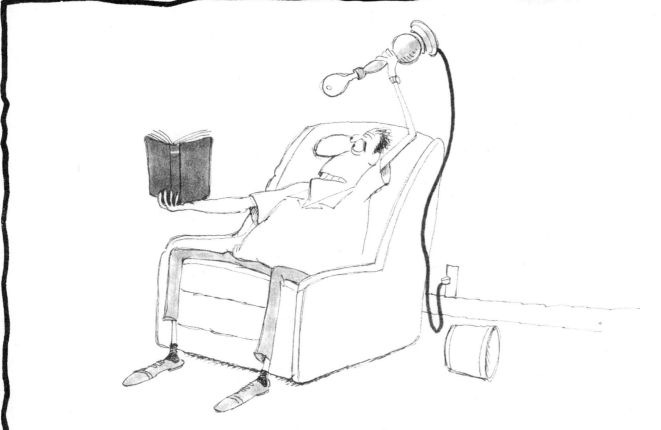

50 HAPPENS.

"I THINK DAD JUST REALIZED THAT HE'S MARRIED TO A GRANDMOTHER."

JUST ABOUT THE TIME YOUR KIDS BECOME WORTH LIVING WITH ...,
THEY'RE LIVING WITH SOMEONE ELSE.

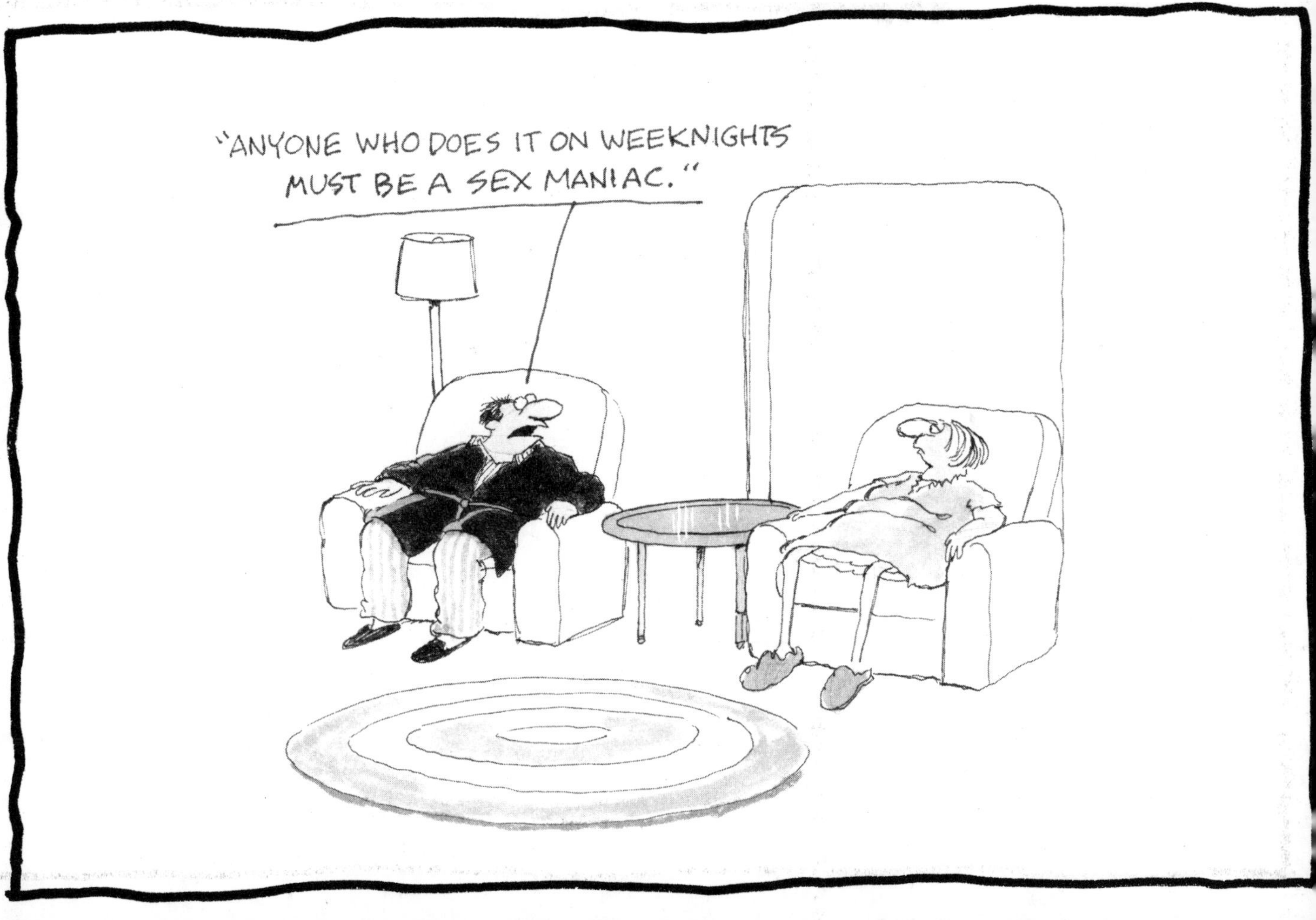
"ANYONE WHO DOES IT ON WEEKNIGHTS MUST BE A SEX MANIAC."

"CERTAIN FOOD JUST ISN'T COMPATIBLE WITH MARYLOU'S GASTROINTESTINAL SYSTEM."
PANCHO'S VILLA

"NO, NO... IT DOESN'T MAKE YOU LOOK FAT."
THAR' SHE BLOWS
THAR' SHE BLOWS
THAR' SHE BLOWS
THAR' SHE BLOWS

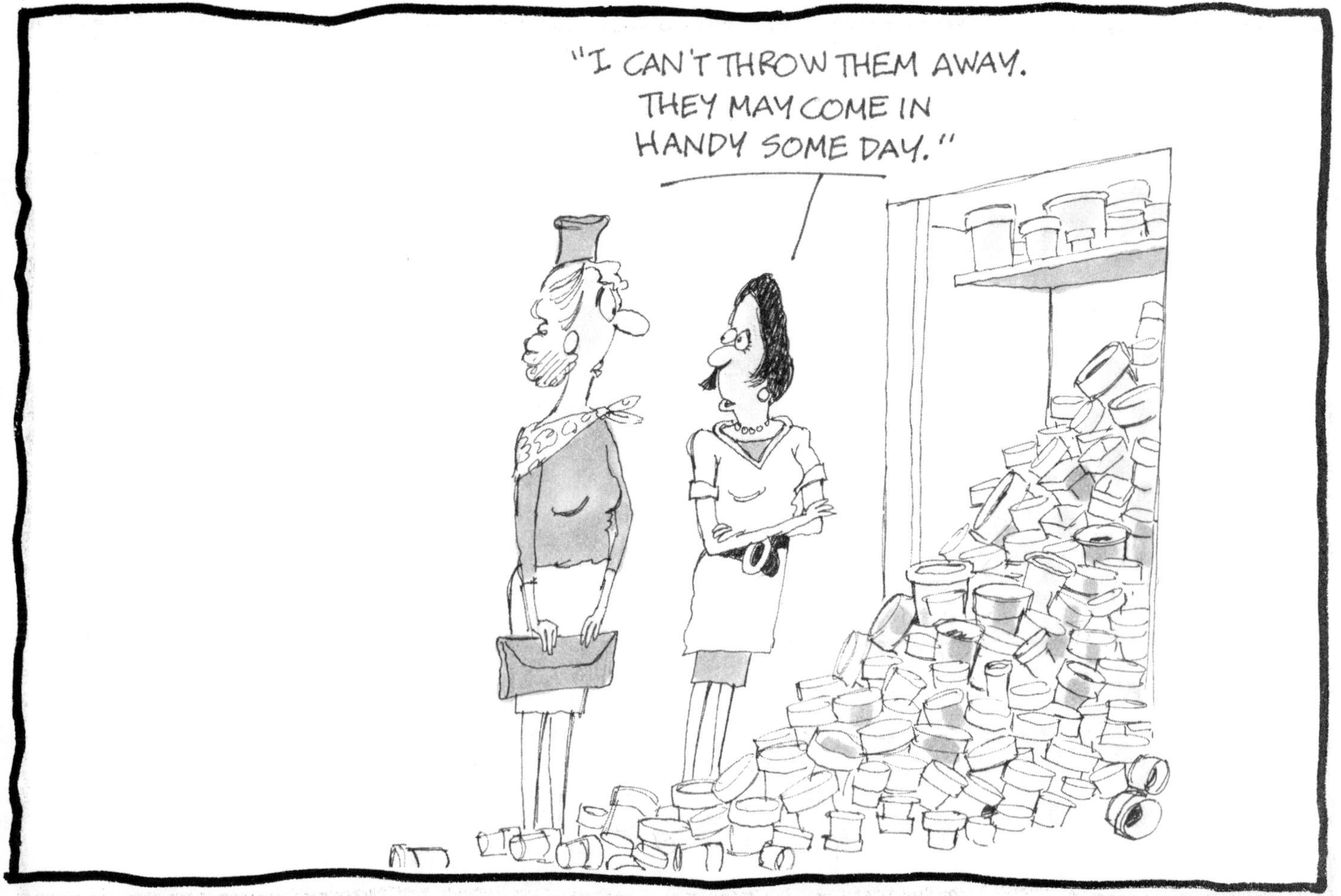
"I CAN'T THROW THEM AWAY. THEY MAY COME IN HANDY SOME DAY."

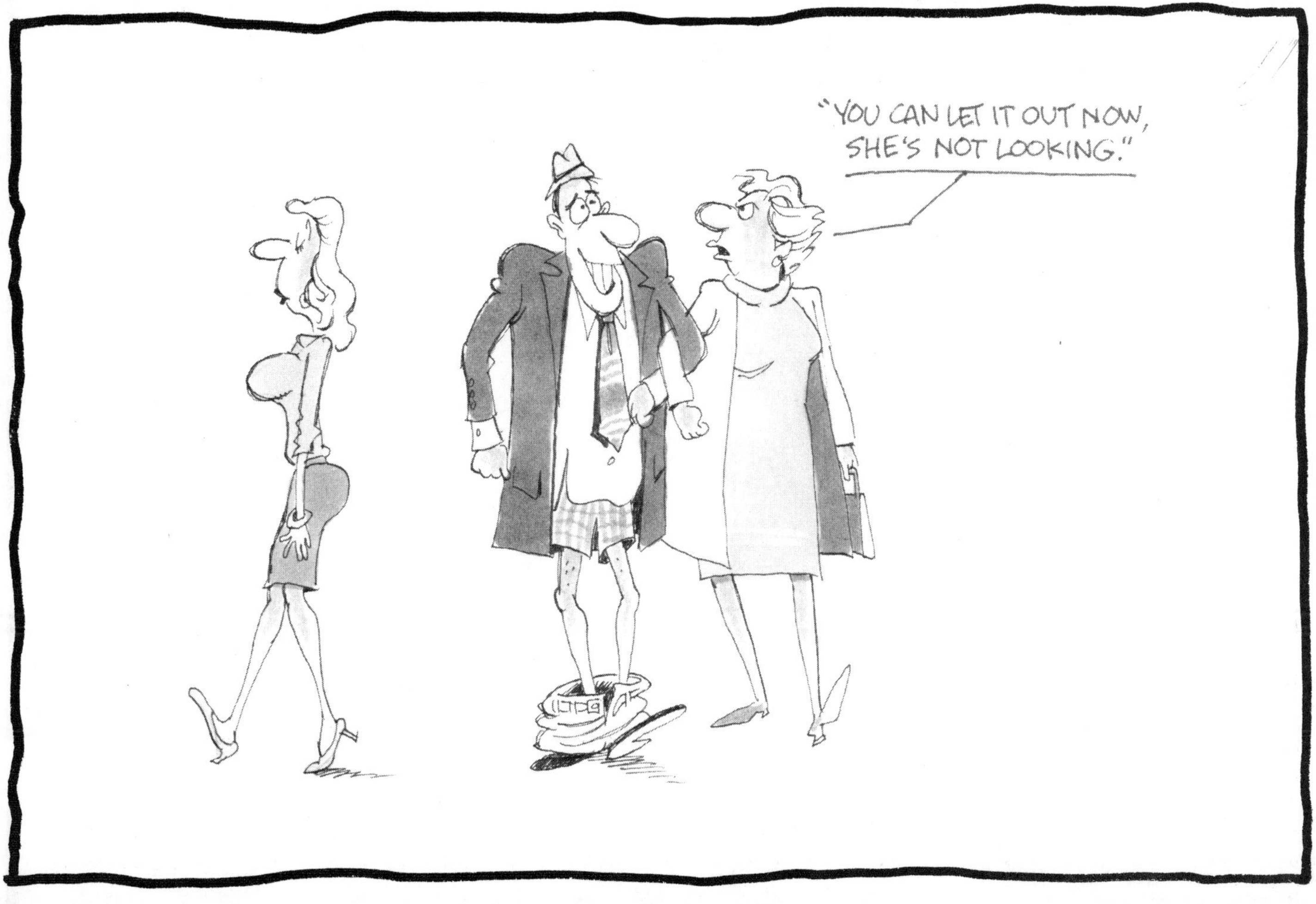
"YOU CAN LET IT OUT NOW,
SHE'S NOT LOOKING."

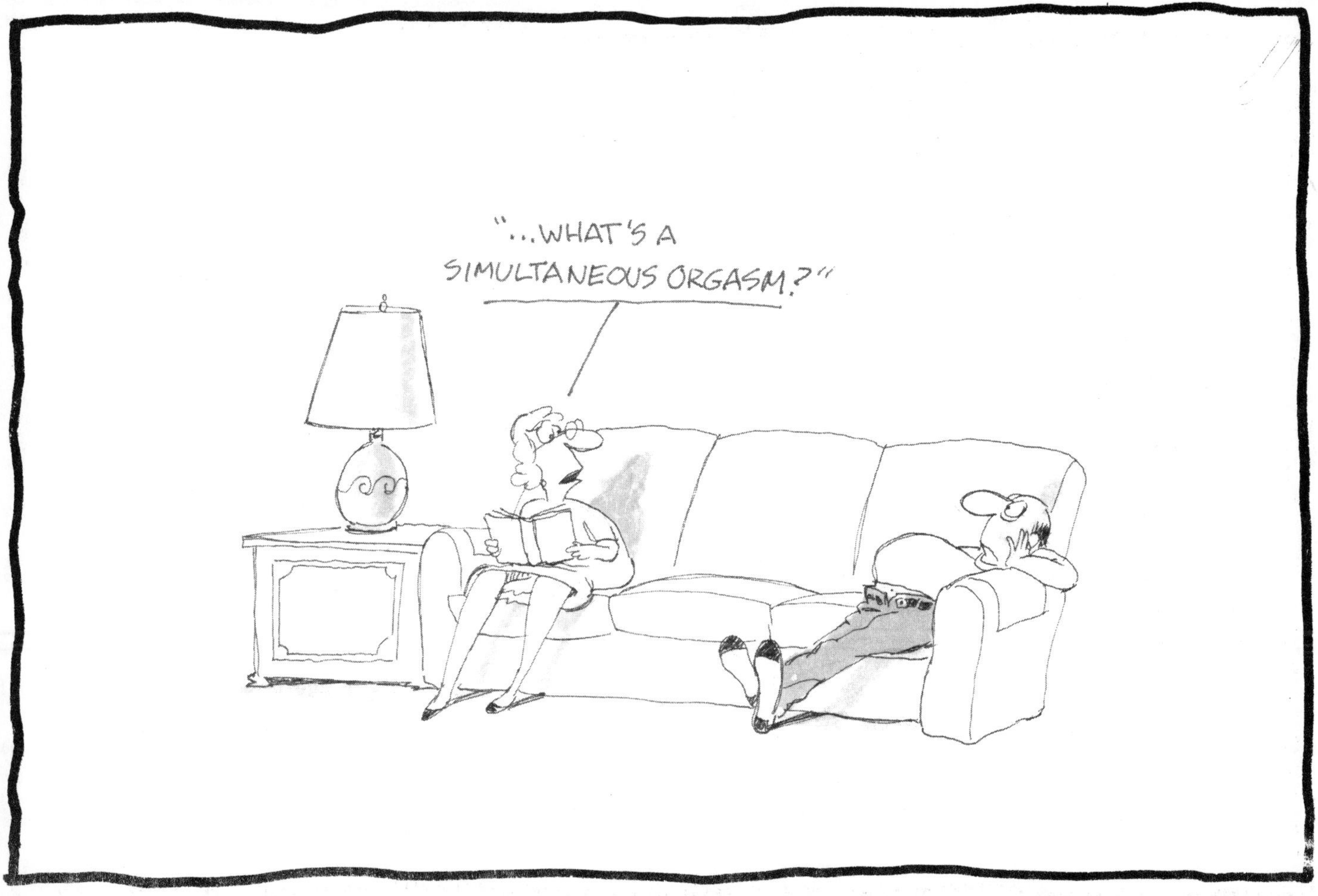
"...WHAT'S A
SIMULTANEOUS ORGASM?"

Other books we publish are available at many fine stores. If you can't find them, send directly to us.

#2400-How To Have Sex On Your Birthday. Finding a partner, special birthday sex positions, places to keep your birthday erection, faking the birthday orgasm, kinky sex on your birthday and much more.

#2401-Is There Sex After Children? There are chapters on pre-teens and privacy, keeping toddlers out of your bedroom, great sex myths to tell your kids, how to have sex on a vacation, places to hide lingerie, where children come from, things kids bring to show and tell and more.

#2402-Confessions From The Bathroom. There are things in this book that happen to all of us that none of us ever talk about. The Gas Station Dump, for example, or the Corn Niblet Dump, the Porta Pottie Dump, the Sunday Newspaper Dump to mention just a few.

#2403-The Good Bonking Guide. Bonking is a great new British term for doing "you know what". Covers bonking in the dark, bonking with foreigners, bonking all night long, improving your bonking, kinky bonking and everything else you've ever wanted (or maybe didn't want) to know.

#2404-Sex Slave: How To Find One, How To Be One. What it takes to be a Sex Slave, how to pick up Sex Slaves, the fine art of sexual groveling, 6 never-fail opening lines and 6 good things to know about break-away clothing -- and more than you ever imagined.

#2405-Mid-Life Sex. Mid-Life Sex is taking all night to do what you used to do all night, talking your wife into visiting a nude beach, being tolerant of farts under the covers and having biological urges dwindle to an occasional nudge.

#2406-World's Sex Records. Lists the greatest sex records of all time, including the world's most successful personal ad, the kinkiest bedroom, the most calories burned during sex, the cheapest escort service and the greatest sex in a car -- plus many more.

#2407-40 Happens. When being out of prune juice ruins your whole day, you finally fulfill your book of the month commitment, you can no longer party for 24 hours straight and you realize anyone with the energy to do it on a weeknight must be a sex maniac.

#2408-30 Happens. When you no longer party all night long, you take out a lifetime membership at your health club, and you still wonder when the baby fat will finally disappear.

#2409-50 Happens. When you remember when "made in Japan" meant something that didn't work, and you can't remember what you went to the top of the stairs for.

#2410-Bosom Buddies. Uncovered at last--the truth about women's bouncy parts: they're probably talking to each other! This book tells us what they would say, if only we could hear them!

#2411-The Geriatric Sex Guide. It's not his mind that needs expanding, and you're in the mood now, but by the time you're naked, you won't be!

#2412-Golf Shots. Humorously tells you how to look for lost balls, what excuses to use to play through first, ways to distract your opponent, and when and where a true golfer is willing to play golf.

#2413-101 Ways to Improve Your Husband Or Wife. Covers how to keep your wife from losing your socks, teaching your husband how to clean a toilet, how to drive your wife crazy, and lots more.

#2414-60 Happens. When your kids start to look middle aged, when software is some kind of comfortable underwear, and when your hearing is perfect if everyone would just stop mumbling.

#2415-Birthdays Happen. When you realize your Mom may not be the greatest cook, when your biological urges dwindle to an occasional nudge, and you realize that your hairline is not receding but that your forehead is growing.

Ivory Tower Publishing Co., Inc.   125 Walnut St., Watertown, MA 02172   (617) 923-1111   **$7.00 postpaid**